Living In Another Time

THE DAYS OF THE CAVE PEOPLE

Living In Another Time

THE DAYS OF THE CAVE PEOPLE

Illustrations by Ginette Hoffman
Text by Françoise Lebrun
Translated by Christopher Sharp

Silver Burdett Company
Morristown, New Jersey and Agincourt, Ontario

Series coordinated by Michel Pierre
in collaboration with Elisabeth Sebaoun

English text consultant:
Professor J.K. Sowards,
Department of History,
Wichita State University

Library of Congress Cataloging-in-Publication Data

Lebrun, Françoise.
The days of the cave people.

(Living in another time)
Translation of: Au temps des cavernes.
Summary: Meruti, a young cave dweller, hunts with the men of his tribe and observes how weapons and tools are made. Sections of the story alternate with brief factual information on aspects of prehistoric life.
1. Man, Prehistoric — Juvenile fiction. [1. Cave dwellers — Fiction. 2. Man, Prehistoric — Fiction]
I. Hoffman, Ginette, ill. II. Title. III. Series:
Des enfants dans l'histoire. English.
PZ7.L47Day 1985 [Fic] 85-40418
ISBN 0-382-09128-0

Published pursuant to agreement with Casterman, Paris
First published in French by Casterman as *Des enfants dans l'Histoire: Au Temps des Cavernes.*

First published in the United States in 1985
by Silver Burdett Company,
Morristown, New Jersey

Published simultaneously in Canada
by GLC/Silver Burdett Publishers

Manufactured in the United States of America

Table of Contents

Page

Meruti's First Hunting Trip

Winter had just begun. At the foot of the hill, grass and lichens could still be seen, poking up through a thin layer of snow. A reindeer was happily grazing on moss and lightly frosted shrubs. The animal had strayed away from the rest of the herd when it came down from the freezing high plateaus. The deer were searching for new grazing grounds.

The reindeer's antlers moved in the air like a bunch of dead branches. Some hunters spotted it from afar. The reindeer was unaware of the three men and the boy who were watching him. They were hidden in the shadows of the pinewoods.

The boy was about ten years old. He had dark eyes and light brown hair that almost reached his shoulders. In his tribe he was called Meruti. That day he was joining the hunters for the first time. Like them he held a spear with a sharp flint point. It could pierce the thickest hides and furs. Like them, he had learned to move about silently in the wilderness, searching for wild game. But up until that day he had only hunted rabbits and birds.

Meruti watched the magnificent animal with the light brown fur as it grazed. It was not aware that danger was so nearby. The boy wondered if he had the strength to throw his spear far enough for it to reach the reindeer.

Tinok, one of the hunters, slowly broke away from the group. Quietly, he crept along the edge of the woods. He wanted to go around the animal and approach it from behind. Then he would be able to drive it toward the others. They waited with their hands tightly grasping the spear throwers that were already loaded with their stone-tipped spears.

Tinok knew that reindeer have a very good sense of smell and very fine hearing. So he could not make the slightest bit of noise or let it feel his presence. But a twig suddenly snapped under Tinok's foot. The reindeer was alerted and stopped grazing. Worried now, it lifted its head and sniffed in all directions. It stood still, ready to escape. Tinok remained motionless and held his breath. For a long while the animal just stood there. Finally, when it had heard no more noise, it bent over once again to eat the delicious lichens.

The hunter approached once more. His feet were covered with hides held together with wide laces. He seemed to glide across the ground. Behind some dwarf willow shrubs, close to the animal, he stopped. Everything was calm. Snowflakes had started to fall lazily. Suddenly, Tinok burst out from behind the brush, shouting.

With a powerful leap the terrified reindeer darted out in front of him. It ran to the edge of the woods where the others waited with their fearsome flint-tipped spears. Tinok threw a spear. It just brushed the animal's side. With terror in its eyes the beast ran faster and faster.

The two other hunters, Mouk and Craal, suddenly came to life. As the reindeer passed in front of them they

threw their weapons. The animal quivered from the shock as the stone tips dug into its side, but it courageously went on. Meruti, who was a little way back, had not yet moved. He had been frightened by the animal's gallop and his companions' voices. Then, in a moment's time, he, too, came to life and threw his weapon. He hit the animal near the right shoulder at its most vulnerable spot. The reindeer was in great pain. It continued on for a few more steps. Then its legs collapsed and it fell down with its muzzle in the snow. The hunters leaped forward and surrounded it. One of them hit the animal over the head with an ax, ending its last jerking movements.

Out of breath and with their hearts pounding, the men looked over their prey. Meruti was filled with emotion and pride. He was the one who had dealt the fatal blow to the animal! He had become a real hunter whom his companions looked upon with respect.

Far off in the distance they could hear the rest of the herd running away from this now dangerous territory. The reindeer that the hunters had killed was a vital catch for their tribe. It was a large male with a huge set of antlers. The tribe needed its meat for food during the winter. Its hide would be used to make clothes. The antlers could be crafted into weapons and its bones into tools. Even its tendons would be used as thread.

Next, the hunters dragged the heavy animal back toward their cave. The women and young children were waiting there. Surely they had heard all the noise and shouting. But they couldn't know that on that frosty morning young Meruti had earned the right to join the hunters in the future.

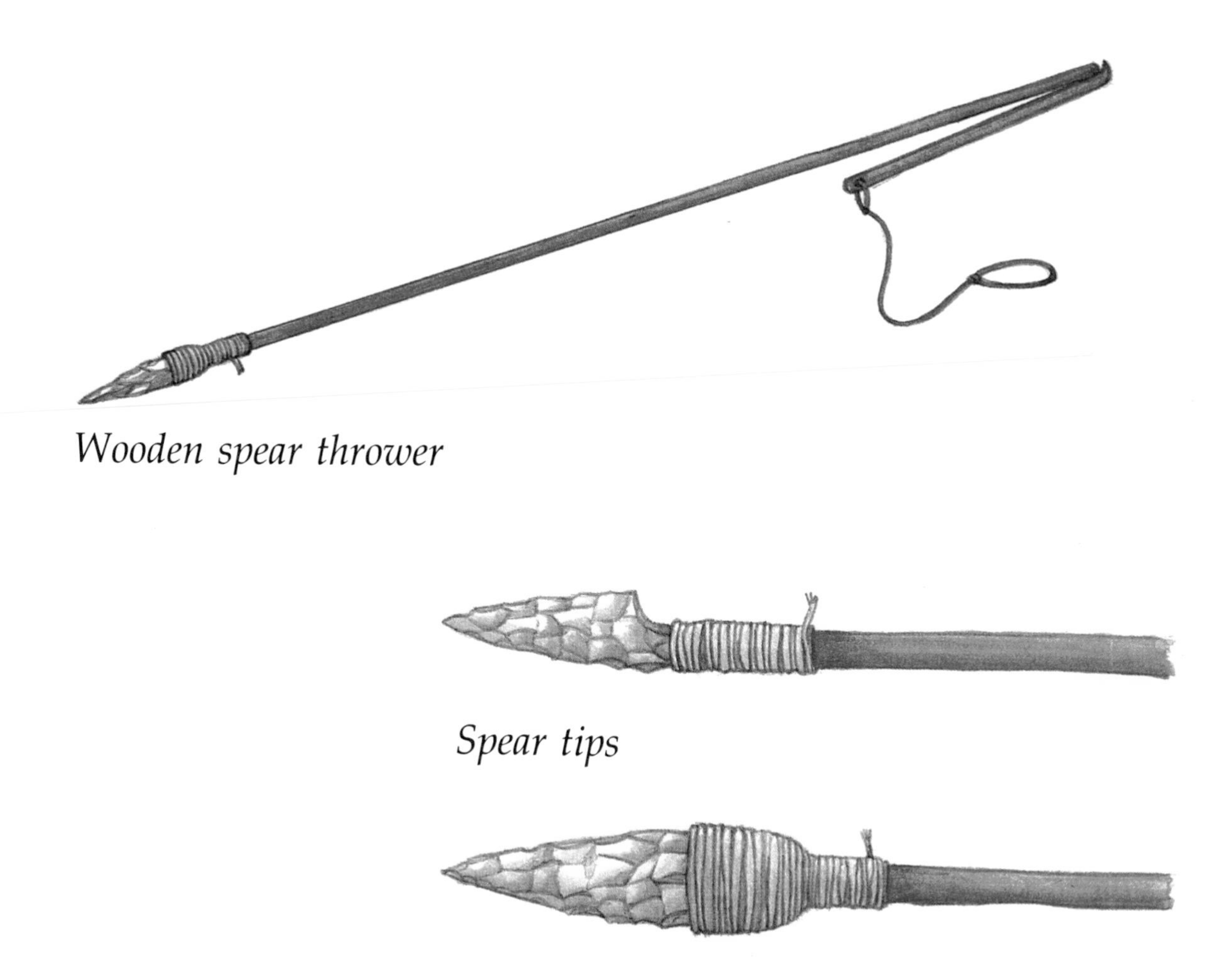

Wooden spear thrower

Spear tips

The Spear and Its Thrower

The first hunters used weapons of crude wooden clubs or made from simple stones. Later, they learned how to chip flint and other hard stones to make sharp, deadly ax blades and spear points.

Almost twenty thousand years ago the spear-thrower was invented. It was made from a piece of reindeer antler and had a hooked end. The spear thrower was attached to the hunter's wrist with a leather strap. A hunter fitted his spear against the hooked end. Next he thrust the thrower forward with a flick of his wrist, making the spear break away with more force. Without the spear thrower hunters could reach targets 150 feet away. With it they could make their spears go twice as far.

The Tribe's Meal

During the warm season Meruti's tribe lived in hide tents. The hunters and their families could easily move these tents from one place to another. In that way, they traveled about searching for wild game. But when the first signs of winter began to appear they all made their way back to their cave. For many, many years they had returned to the same spot in winter to protect themselves from the cold.

The cave was large and deep. Its entrance was protected by a rocky overhang at the foot of a cliff. From the opening they could see the valley below.

In the middle of the cave a fire was always burning. The hearth where the fire burned had been dug in the ground and was surrounded by a circle of flat stones. Two women and two children were warming themselves by the fire when they were startled by a noise from outside.

"It's Meruti!" shouted one of the children.

Everyone ran out of the cave, roughly pushing aside the skin that hung over the entrance. At the bottom of the path that led to the cave they could see the hunting party returning.

"They killed a reindeer!" exclaimed one woman.

"Just look at how big it is!" said another woman. "We can get lots of meat from it and make new clothes with its skin."

The reindeer was laid down in front of the cave so that everyone could see it. The eldest hunter, Mouk, slowly told how Meruti had dealt the fatal blow to the wild animal. When the story was finished the men and women took some sharp cutting flints from a pile in a corner of the cave. They went to work on the reindeer, cutting away a few strips of meat to have for their evening meal.

Meruti carried the meat over to the hearth where Taori, the youngest woman of the group, roasted it over the glowing embers. "I'll also have to teach you how to braise meat," she said to Meruti as she tended to the meal. "First you dig a hole in the ground and line it with glowing red stones from the fire. Then you lay some small game on it, like snow partridges, and you cover the game up with another layer of hot stones. When the stones begin to cool down you take them off and put new ones down. That way the meat cooks very slowly and takes on a special flavor. It's very, very good."

While Meruti was listening to Taori another woman, Naoki, had taken some red, glowing stones from the hearth. She placed them on a wooden board to carry them and then dropped the stones into a skin pouch filled with water, grains, and dried mushrooms. The hot stones heated the water and it soon began to simmer, letting off a thin, white cloud of steam. After a short time, everyone was able to fill up their bone or wooden bowls with this hot, sweet smelling liquid.

By now the whole tribe was gathered around the hearth. Two small children, Tiki and Rok, went from one hunter to the next, eating pieces of meat from their portions. When the children were full they began playing flutes made from hollowed out bird bones with holes drilled in them.

Then Craal began playing low notes from a bigger flute that he had made out of a reindeer antler. It also had been hollowed out, and three perfectly round and polished holes had been made in it.

After awhile the strange music stopped. No one was laughing or talking any longer. The silence allowed each person to enjoy the warmth from the hearth and the delightful feeling of having a full stomach.

Tiki and Rok were soon bundled off to bed in heavy furs. Meruti was very tired from the morning's hunt and should have gone to sleep, too. But he fought off the desire to sleep and thought about his first successful hunt. The boy was pleased with himself, but knew that more difficult experiences lay ahead of him. He would soon be expected to hunt animals more dangerous and ferocious than reindeer.

Fire

Learning how to make fire was one of the most important discoveries in history. Historians of early humans believe that the discovery of fire was made about 400,000 years ago. This belief is based on datings made from hearth remains found at several sites.

In prehistoric times there were two ways to make fire. In the first method one piece of flint was struck against another to make sparks. The second method required a dry stick that was rapidly twirled around in a hole made in a softer piece of wood. Friction caused the wood to heat up, and dry moss was kept nearby to be lit.

A Boy is Found

The following day the hunters checked to see that their flint stones were sharp enough. Then, with confident, precise strokes, they began to skin the animal. The women took the large pieces of skin that came off and vigorously stretched them out. They spread them out on the ground and attached them to large pegs driven into the earth. Meruti stood nearby and watched everyone while they worked.

"You see Meruti, we have to scrape away every bit of fat and flesh that are on the reindeer skin," Taori explained.

"Why?" the boy asked.

"When pieces of flesh are left on the hide they can damage it by making it rot."

"Besides, we need all the fat," Naoki added. "You know, the stone lamps that give us light don't work by magic. Each lamp has a wick that's been coated with fat so it will burn for a long time."

Kneeling down, Taori and Naoki skillfully handled the scrapers. It wasn't long before a large section of the skin was cleaned. Then it was put in the cave to dry. Other hides, prizes from earlier hunting trips, had dried by then. Naoki looked them over, chose two, and sat down to make a piece of clothing. With a flint awl she made several holes along the edges of the two hides. Then, with reindeer tendons, she sewed them together, leaving openings for the head and each arm.

Soon the reindeer was no more than a skeleton. But each and every one of its bones would be used, right down to the last one. Mouk, Craal, and Tinok looked over the animal's antlers. They were already dreaming of the spears, throwers, tool handles, and even the flutes they would carve from these magnificent antlers.

Meruti wandered away from the rest of the group. Earlier that morning he had recovered his stone-tipped spear that had lodged in the reindeer's shoulder. His weapon had been damaged. The flint point had moved from where it had been attached to the spear's shaft. The boy got some dry tendons and began to repair his spear. Now that he was a hunter he had to take care of his weapon.

Suddenly, the boy set down his weapon. He ran to the side of the cliff and huddled up in a corner. The others in the group were not surprised by Meruti's odd behavior. They just watched him without saying a word. Everyone remembered when the tribe had found him almost a year earlier.

Meruti had been living on his own for some time. During a bear hunt his father had been wounded. He had not survived the beast's fierce attack. Meruti had dug a hole in the ground for his father's grave. Around the body he placed seashell ornaments, his father's weapons, and a few flower petals. He then covered the body with heavy stones to keep animals from tearing it apart.

While living on his own the boy had managed to survive even though he had no fire, and only crude weapons which were not very effective. He had protected himself from wolf packs, charging aurochs (wild oxen), and clawing bears. He had only eaten when he was able to catch hares, small foxes, or trout that he caught with his hands. At night he had slept alone in caves that he came upon. Surviving grew more difficult as the weather got colder. But then one day Mouk had found him, nearly starving and numb with cold.

Since then he had lived with Mouk's people. Meruti was happy that he had found a new family. From time to time though he still went off by himself. No one was ever surprised. While the members of his new family found Meruti mysterious, they also found that he was a valuable addition to the tribe. The boy understood nature better than anyone else. Some members of the tribe even believed that Meruti was destined to one day take over Mouk's place as the shaman (priest or medicine-man) of the tribe.

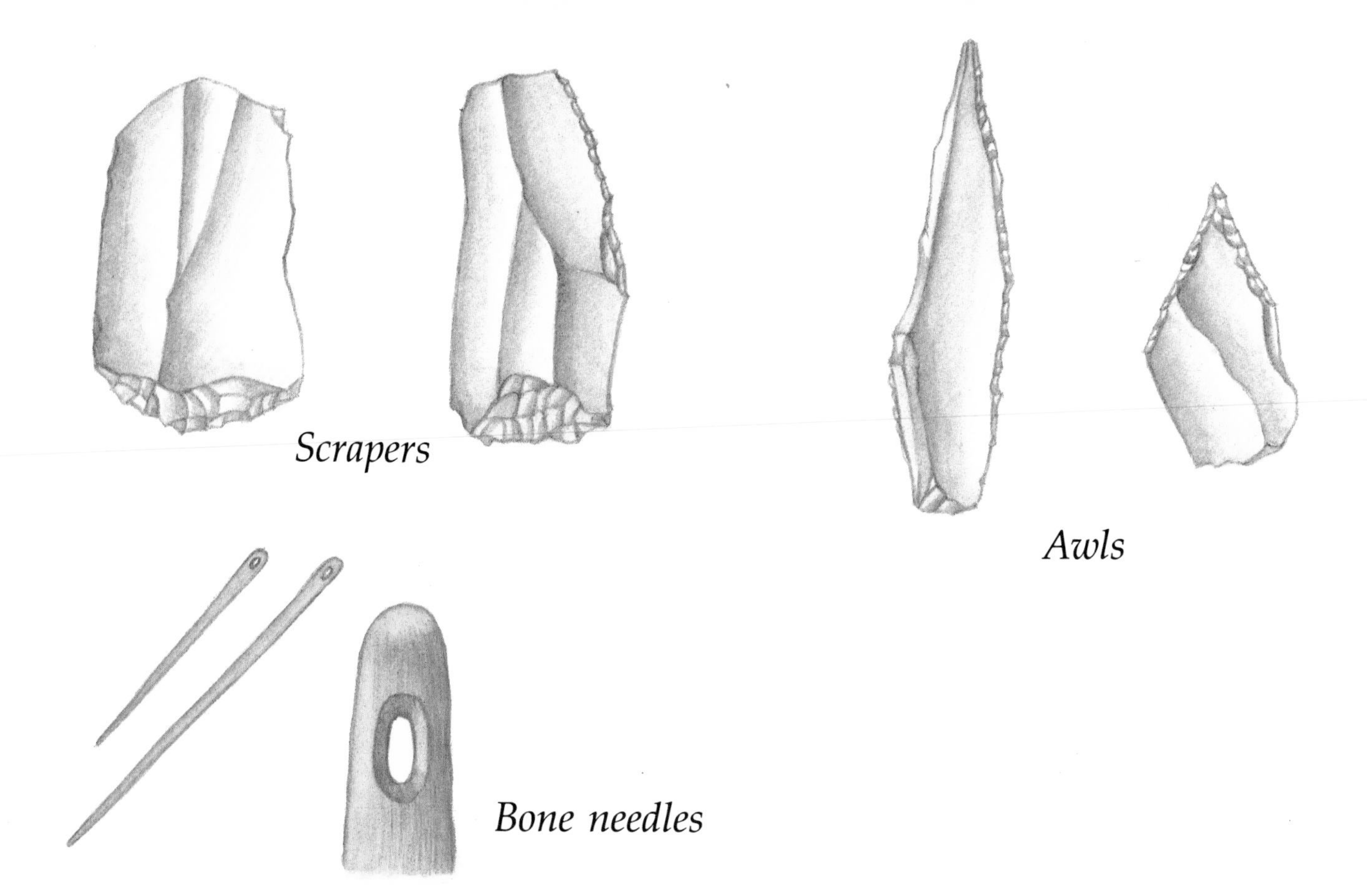

Hides and Furs

Hundreds of thousands of years went by before people were able to make clothes. In places where the weather was warm they lived without clothes. But in areas where the weather was cold they needed something to keep them warm. At first people just used animal skins and furs to protect themselves from the cold. In time they learned how to cut and sew furs and skins to make real clothes.

To do this they used scrapers, awls, and needles. The thread they used was made from horse hair or from dried nerves or tendons that had been cut into fine strips.

All these tools had been perfected by the period in time known as the *Magdalenian* phase—between 15,000 and 10,000 B.C. This period was named after the Madeleine cave in Dordogne, France. It is one of the largest prehistoric sites in France.

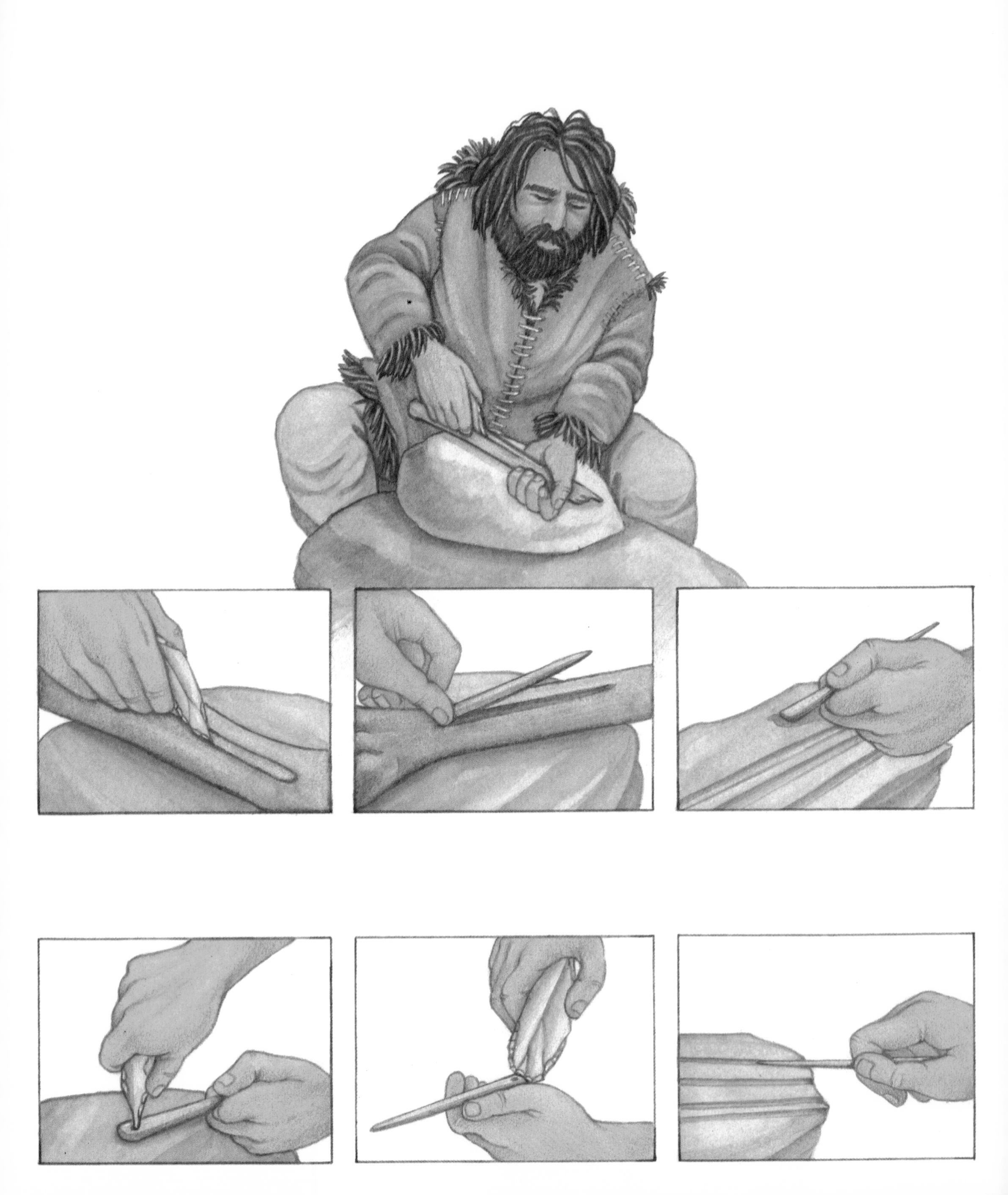

The Flint Tool Maker

Tinok sat in front of the cave. In his lap was a big tibia bone from a reindeer. He picked up a flint burin and traced the shape of a needle in the bone. With great precision he cut and dug into the bone. Then, with the pressure of his thumb, he made the needle pop out. He took it in his hands and polished it by rubbing it against a rock. Next with the tip of a small flint tool called an awl, he made a hole in the needle. He had made a needle with an eye. This was very useful for sewing skins together to make clothing.

Tinok could also make barbed harpoons, spear points, and fishhooks. Once Meruti had even seen him turn the shoulder blade of a reindeer into a shovel. Tinok was also a talented artist. He could sculpt horses' heads or women's bodies out of pieces of bone or ivory mammoth tusks.

While Tinok liked to work with bone and ivory, Mouk was very good at making stone tools. During the warm season he went to spots that only he knew of and searched for large flint blocks. He carried these back to the cave and carefully stored them. Mouk used them later to make tools as they were needed by his tribe.

By studying the chipped flint stones found in digs archaeologists have pieced together the methods used by our ancestors to make tools. Some fifteen thousand years later they have been able to recreate the way in which weapons and tools were made in prehistoric times. At this period in time, Mouk was sitting in front of the cave under Meruti's admiring gaze.

Mouk could make many different kinds of tools—end scrapers, round scrapers, awls, or burins. His motions were so precise and quick that it only took him a few moments for him to finish a piece.

He had learned his skills from his father, who had learned them from his father and so on down the line. But with each new generation progress was made. Every new idea brought about little improvements in the technique of shaping flint stones and in the finished product. Mouk was always trying to make better tools. He was the person in the tribe whom Meruti looked up to the most. The boy never grew bored with watching him work on the flint tools.

"You see," Mouk said to him, "the most important thing to do before you begin is to make sure the flint stone is not cracked or fractured."

"How do you do that?" Meruti asked.

"I hit it with a rock and listen to the sound it makes. If it makes a muffled sound, the flint block is cracked and cannot be used. But, if it makes a clear sound, I know it can be used."

"And then what?"

"Using a very hard rock, I strike my stone block. If I hit it in the right place, a large blade of flint will fall away."

"And if you don't hit it in the right place?"

"Then the flint could break up into many useless pieces."

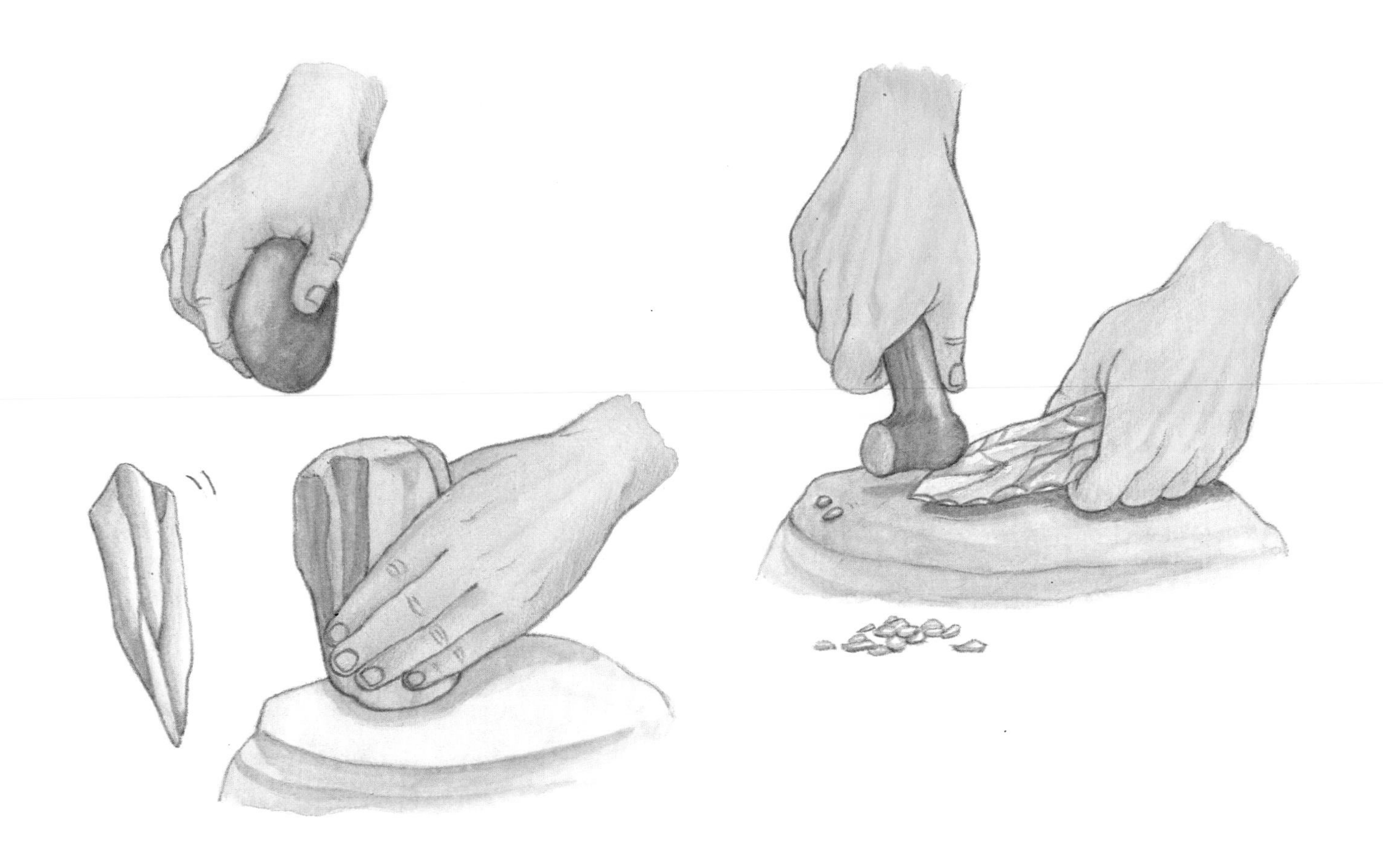

As he spoke, Mouk struck the stone block. With one blow a blade of flint fell to the ground. He picked it up, looked it over, and ran his fingers over the rough edges. Next, he took a piece of reindeer antler and made many light blows to the blade's edge. As he worked, small chips of stone broke away and fell to the ground around his feet.

Little by little, right in front of Meruti's eyes, a thin and finely shaped blade appeared. It was almost possible to see through the edges. The blade looked like a large laurel leaf. More than a tool, it had now become a work of art.

Meruti was amazed by what he had just seen. He left Mouk to his work and went inside the cave. The boy sat down next to Craal who had placed some seashells and the teeth from all sorts of animals down on a big rock. Craal picked up some teeth from a wolf he had killed at the beginning of the cold season. One by one he pierced each tooth at its root end with an awl. Then he strung them up on a leather lace. Meruti knew how to make the same kind of necklace, but he was waiting to have killed his first wolf and later his first bear before daring to wear one.

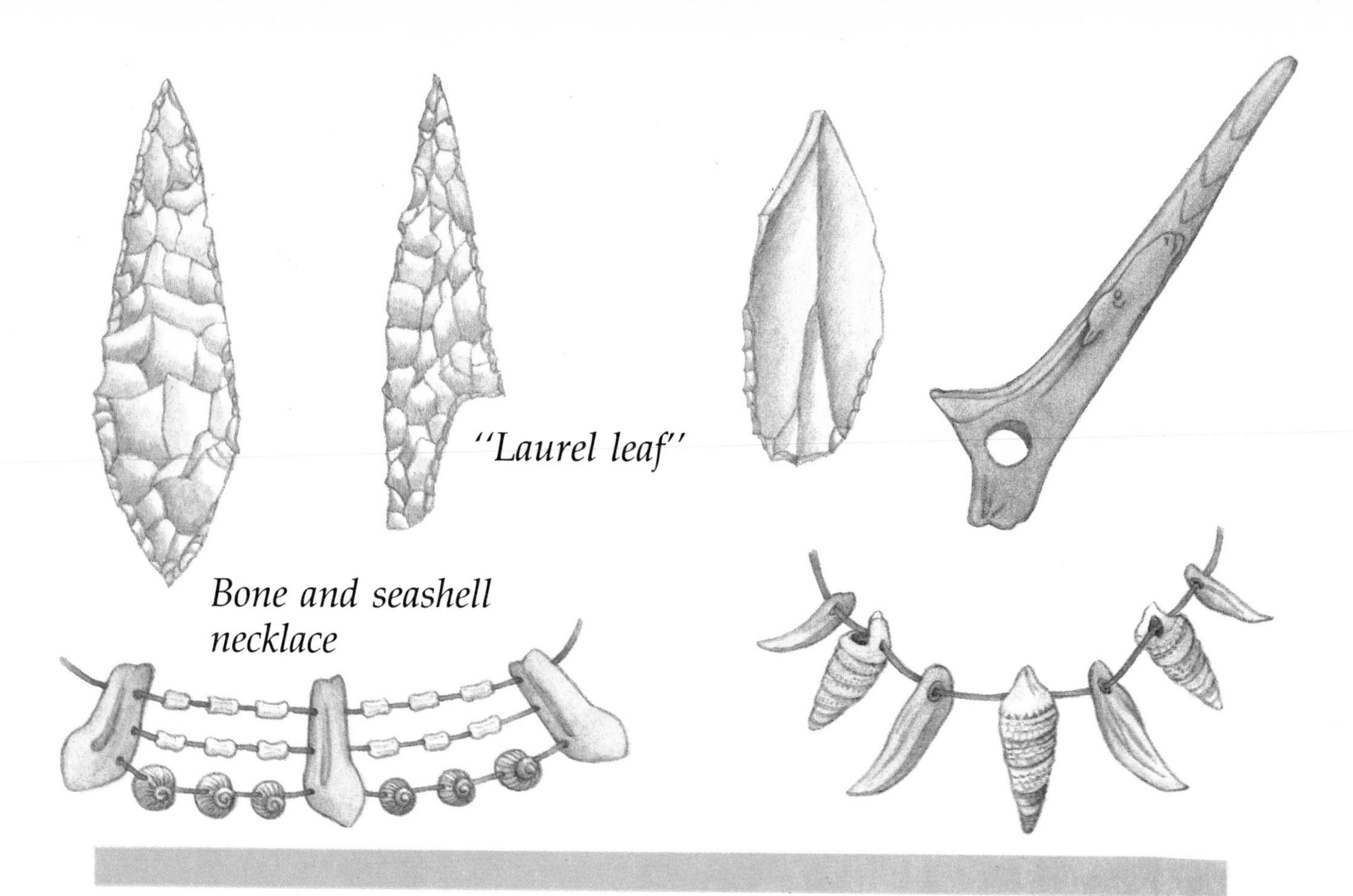

Using Flint

Flint was the hardest stone used in prehistoric times. In the beginning, over two million years ago, the stones used were only roughly shaped at one end. Then, over a period of several thousand years, people learned ways to shape the stones on both sides and make them very sharp. Then the stones they made could be used in many different ways. Flint could be found almost everywhere. People took it away in blocks. From these many kinds of tools could be made. From one stone block, a stonecutter could make several blades as well as some scrapers, awls, and even spear points when this art was invented in about 10,000 B.C.

The most beautifully crafted stones that have been found from prehistoric times are those shaped like the laurel leaf (and have the same name). Measuring about twelve inches in length, they are so fine that their edges are almost transparent. We do not know what possible use they could have had in prehistoric times because they seem much too fragile to have been used as tools. Maybe even then they were simply considered works of art?

The Secrets of the Cave

The flames from the fire made huge, dancing shadows on the cave walls. Almost everyone was sleeping peacefully. But not Meruti, he was wide awake and waiting. Something had intrigued him the night before. He had seen Mouk leave the cave after the others were asleep. Meruti had watched him as he walked away, holding a torch to light his way. Mouk was carrying some small leather pouches. In them the boy thought he had seen some different colored powders.

Tonight Meruti was watching Mouk again. He wanted to follow the older man but he didn't know if he was bold enough. Suddenly, the boy trembled with excitement. Mouk had gotten up. Like an animal on the alert Meruti watched him, following the man's every move. He saw Mouk gather together black pieces of stone. Then he picked up a branch with animal hair tied to one end. Mouk took a resin torch and lit it from the fire in the hearth. But he didn't go toward the cave opening. Instead, he walked toward Meruti. Mouk gave the boy a piece of sandstone that had been hollowed out in the middle. "Here Meruti," he said quietly, "take this and follow me."

The boy got up, his heart racing with excitement. He took the strange object and held it tightly against his chest. Mouk and Meruti left the cave and went out into the cold night. The freezing air took their breath away. They walked very quickly. It wasn't long before they entered another cave. This cave was quite near to their own, but smaller and much deeper. They slipped through a narrow passage and arrived in a large room.

Mouk walked slowly up to one wall. When the light from the torch lit the wall Meruti cried out with surprise. The wall was covered with many drawings and paintings. There were bison, horses, and reindeer that all seemed to be running along the wall. Even on the ceiling animals galloped past each other. Meruti could not tear himself away from the forms and colors he saw before his eyes. He could almost hear the animals whinny or bleat!

One creature interested him more than the others. It was a mammoth with huge tusks. Long, shaggy hair flowed down its back. He remembered seeing a mammoth once. It was while he had been living alone after his father died. These huge beasts scared him. But Meruti knew it was possible to lure them into traps and then kill them with spears and stones. Mouk had even explained to him that at one time mammoth tusks had been used as tent frames. Their ancestors drove the large ends of the tusks into the ground. The pointed ends were joined together at the top and hides were placed over them to form a shelter.

"Meruti, come over here and hold the torch for me!" Mouk said. He handed the boy the torch and picked up a piece of black stone.

He began to draw lines and curves. Meruti was speechless as he saw a reindeer slowly come to life on

the wall. It was as magnificent as the one they had hunted down that other morning. Next, in the sandstone bowl, Mouk placed a bit of crushed red clay and some grease. He carefully mixed these ingredients together. Then Mouk said, "Meruti, hand me that stick with the reindeer hair please."

Meruti handed it to him, wondering what he was going to do with it. Mouk took the strange object and dipped it in the red liquid. Then he filled in a bison's head with the color. It was next to the reindeer that he had just drawn. From time to time, he picked up the black stone again and added a detail or two to the animal. Every so often Mouk stepped back to judge his work.

Many artists before him had also painted on the walls of this cave. Each generation had added its own creations to those the previous one had drawn. Mouk knew that he was the inheritor of a tradition. This tradition entrusted each tribe's shaman with the job of decorating the caves.

The torch soon burned down. The light had grown dim. Mouk picked up his tools from the cave floor. "Come on Meruti, we'll go home now."

They both went back out into the cold. It wasn't long before they were back in their own cave. Wrapped in his fur and trying to sleep, Meruti could still imagine the large herds of the night.

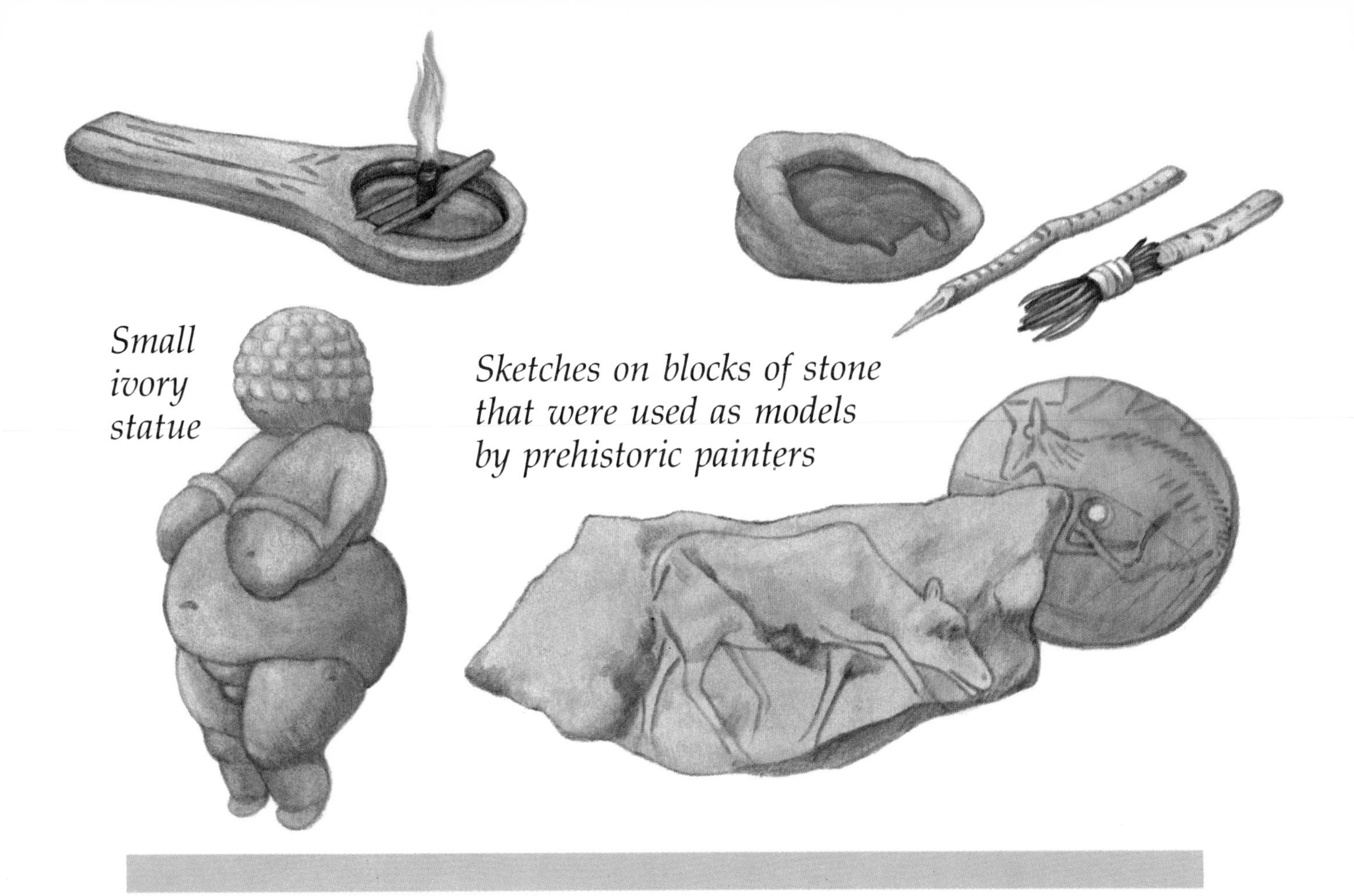

Small ivory statue

Sketches on blocks of stone that were used as models by prehistoric painters

The First Artists

Prehistoric artists decorated caves to turn them into sanctuaries. Ceremonies that were held to initiate young hunters probably took place in these caves.

The painters frequently drew animals, but rarely human faces or forms. The colors they used (ochre, brown, red, and black) came from rocks or naturally colored earth. In order to paint, they used their fingers or animal hair paint brushes.

In these dark caves the artists needed light to work by. They used resin torches or lamps made from small sandstone blocks with oil covered wicks.

Among the other works of art left to us from prehistoric times are small figures sculpted from bone or ivory. The most flourishing period of prehistoric art was between 35,000 and 10,000 B.C.

The Winter Salmon

The fire glowed red in the darkness of the night. From time to time, the howling of wolves broke through the silence. The scent of humans and of the reindeer carcass attracted them. Yet they did not dare to come near the cave.

In the cave both young and old were curled up in their furs and sound asleep. Everyone except for Meruti, who was rolled up in a bear skin, unable to sleep. He kept thinking about all the painted animals he had discovered in the other cave. In his mind he could still picture them. He wanted to go back to look at them more. He was afraid, though, that in the darkness he wouldn't be able to find his way. Besides, without Mouk, he might have been a little afraid!

The most beautiful image in his mind was that of the salmon he had seen painted on the wall. He remembered its slender body and pointed mouth. Salmon were Meruti's favorite creatures. He loved the silvery, bluish color of these big fish. He always admired their leaps and bounds as they swam back up the river's rapids.

When the tribe had first taken him in Meruti showed them where they could find the best fishing spots. Most importantly of all, he always seemed to know the exact moment when the salmon would return.

How did he always guess correctly? Even he did not know. The time he had spent alone in the wilderness had helped him learn many things. During that time he developed his power of observation. He had also gained a greater sensitivity to nature.

It was very early in the morning. Meruti was the first one to wake up. Something made him get up and leave the cave. It was just a feeling the boy had. Wrapped in his fur clothes he stood very still and looked out over the mist covered landscape. He could hardly see the bottom of the cliff where the river was. Suddenly, Meruti rushed down the path that led to the river. When he reached the water's edge, breathlessly he climbed up on a large rock. His senses were sharp. For a long time he did not move a muscle. He just sat there and followed the moving water with his eyes. Suddenly he saw shadows in the water. He looked carefully. He was sure he saw them. He did —they were the salmon, the first ones that winter! Immediately he jumped up and quickly climbed down from the rock. Then he raced back to the cave shouting, "Salmon! Salmon!"

He was still shouting the good news when he entered the cave. Everyone else was awake now and they jumped from their warm beds. Mouk looked at the boy with surprise. Once again Meruti was the one to announce the return of the salmon. The men grabbed their harpoons and followed Meruti. He was already running back down the path to the river.

From the bank of the river the sight was wonderful. The big fish dodged in and out, swimming against the

current and leaping over the rapids. Each time the fish leaped into the air Mouk, Tinok, and Craal threw their harpoons. Sometimes they were lucky, and speared a fish. But often their harpoons landed harmlessly in the water. They carried the fish they did catch to the riverbank. There, the women and children clubbed each fish over the head to end its suffering.

The fishing party was a great success. Everyone rejoiced. The day's catch of salmon, along with the reindeer meat would provide the tribe with plenty of food for the winter months. Meruti was very happy. He was pleased and proud that he had been able to help his tribe by using his skills as a hunter and fisherman.

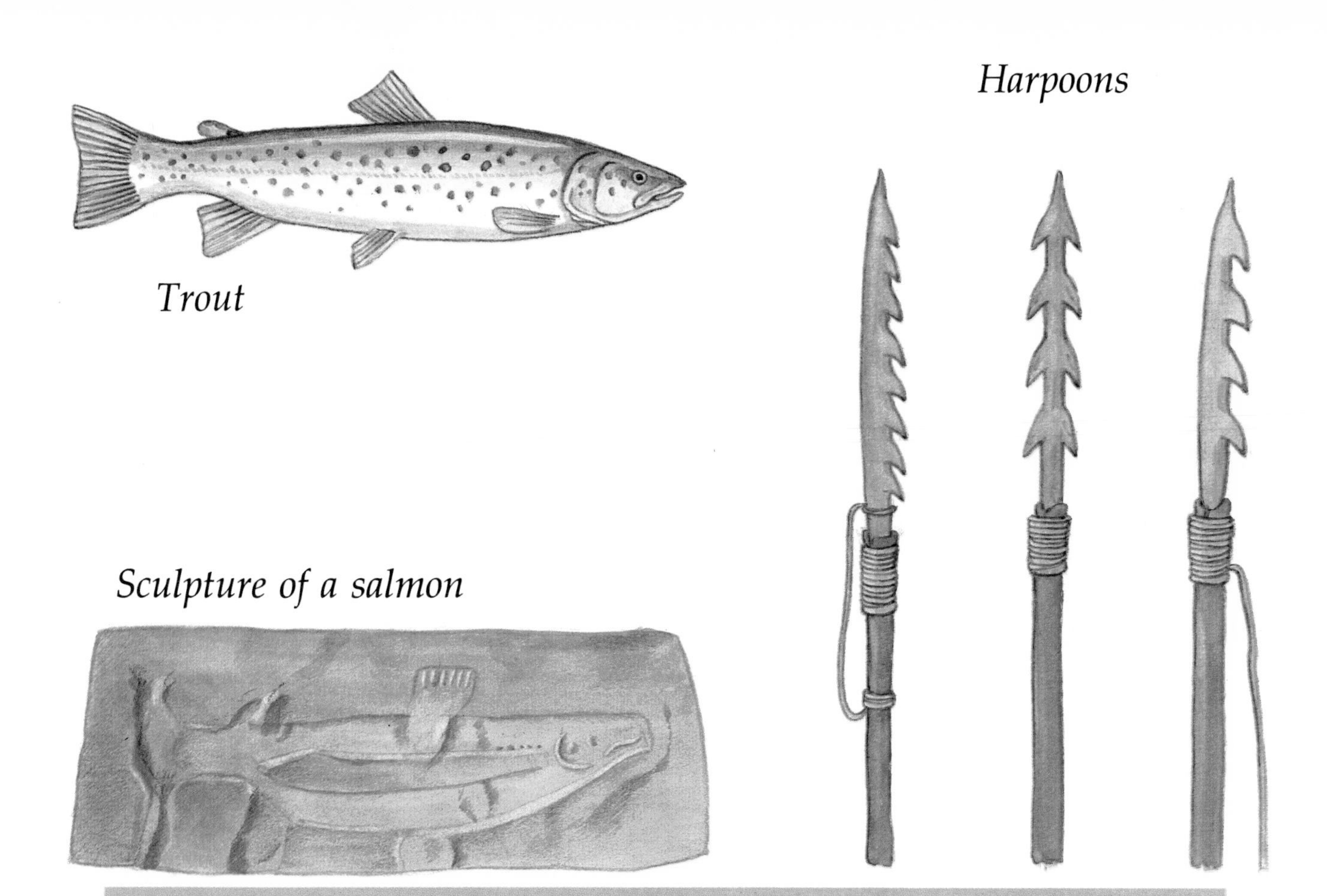
Trout

Harpoons

Sculpture of a salmon

Harpoons and Fishhooks

For hundreds of thousands of years prehistoric people lived by hunting, gathering wild plants, and fishing. Salmon, pike, perch, and eels were the most prized river fish. People who lived near the sea also fished. They gathered shellfish mainly—mussels, limpets, abalones, and oysters.

Fishing methods improved greatly when the harpoon was invented in about 15,000 B.C. It was carved out of bone and equipped with barbs. When it was attached to a wooden shaft the harpoon was a very efficient weapon. Skillfully thrown, it could catch fish swimming near the water's surface or in shallow streams.

At about the same time a type of fishhook was invented. It was made out of bone, sharpened on both ends, attached to a strap. As soon as a fish bit the bait on the hook, the bone went down its throat. All that was left for the fisherman to do was to pull his catch out of the water with the strap.

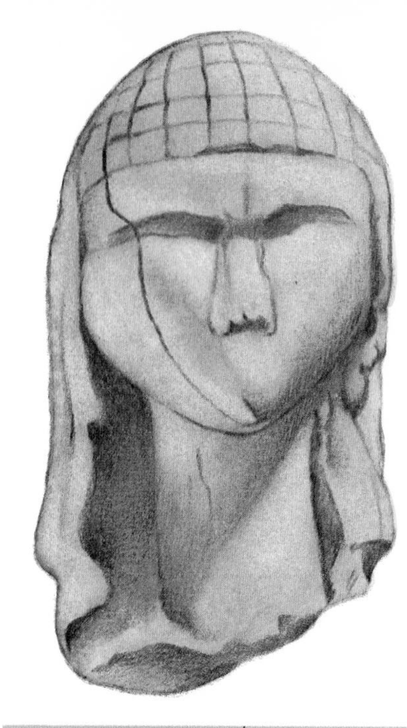

The Venus of Brassempouy:
The first sculpture of a human face

Where Can Prehistoric People Still be Found?

In Museums

Most natural history museums have exhibits related to the times of the cave people. You can check in your school or public library for the location of a nearby natural history museum. If you live near or plan to visit New York, Chicago, or Washington, D.C. perhaps you can spend some time in one of the museums in the list below.

The American Museum of Natural History (New York)

The Field Museum of Natural History (Chicago)

The Smithsonian Institution, The National Museum of Natural History (Washington, D.C.)

In Caves

Lascaux (Dordogne, France): This is the most beautifully painted cave from prehistoric times. It was first discovered in 1940 and was opened to visitors until 1963. The hundreds of paintings (dating from 35,000 to 15,000 B.C.) had begun to deteriorate because of the passage of the thousands of tourists who flocked to the site each year. In 1984, an artificial cave, built near the original one, was opened to the public. Reproductions of the original paintings are displayed there.

Animals and Humans

Human beings appeared on earth four million years ago. Since then they have encountered and hunted many different animals. But they never lived during the same time period as the dinosaurs as is sometimes believed. The last dinosaurs disappeared almost 200 million years ago.

In reality, the animals that people have encountered during their thousands of years of existence look very much the same as those we are familiar with today. A few big mammals have died out though. One of these is the mammoth which disappeared about 12,000 years ago.

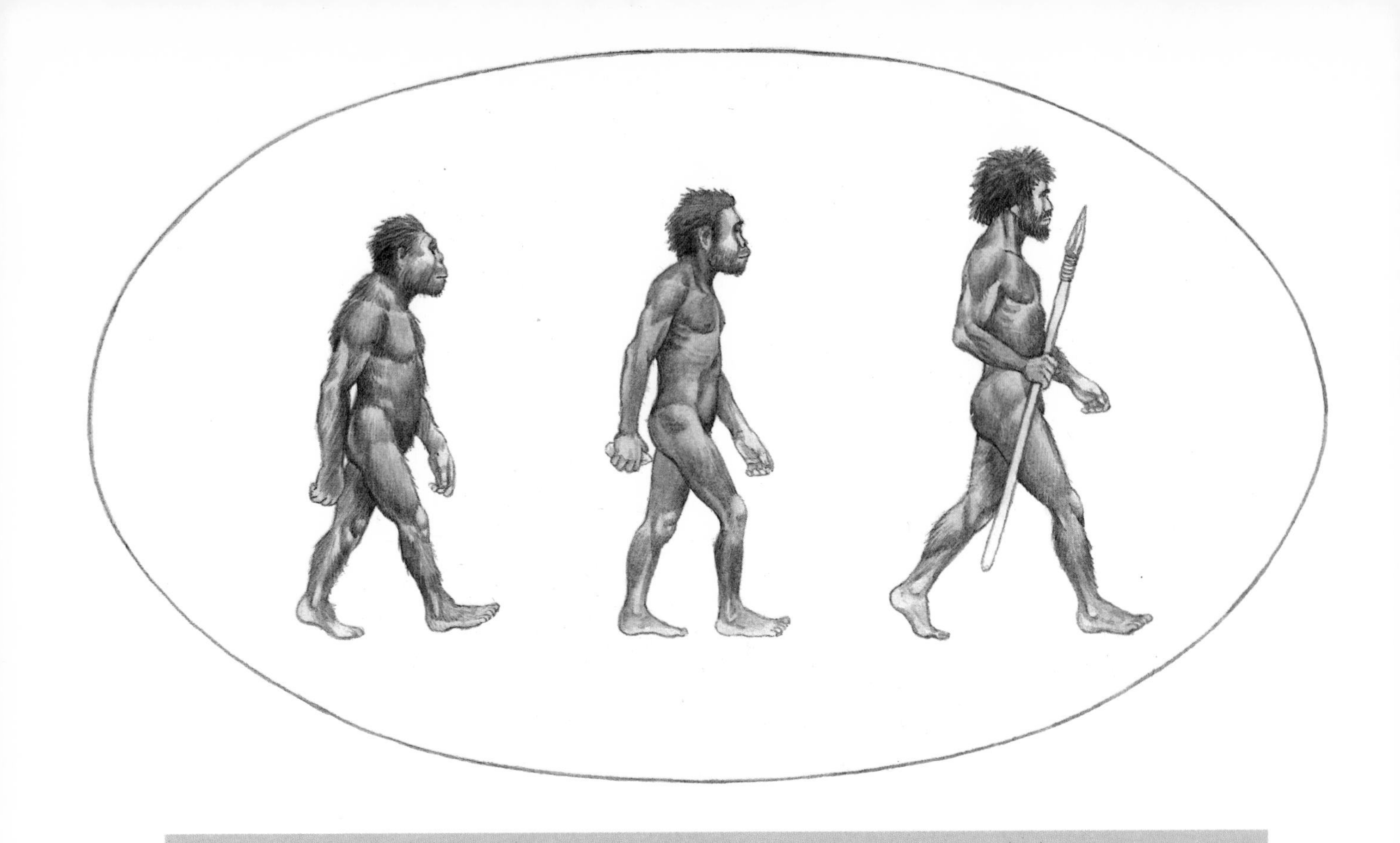

Our Origins

The earth has existed for **5 billion years**.

The first living cells appeared, in the sea, **3 billion years** ago.

The first aquatic animals with a vertebral column date back **500 million years**. Little by little, slowly and progressively, their fins turned to feet.

The first quadraped animal with thirty-two teeth was born **35 million years** ago.

Our earliest ancestors date back about **4 million years**. They were small bipeds (less than 4 feet tall) originating from austral Africa, who hunted and gathered grains and made crude tools.

People learned how to make fire **400,000 years** ago.

For the past **100,000 years**, they have practiced burial rituals. They began making elaborate stone, bone, and wooden tools and creating wonderful works of art **20,000 years** ago.

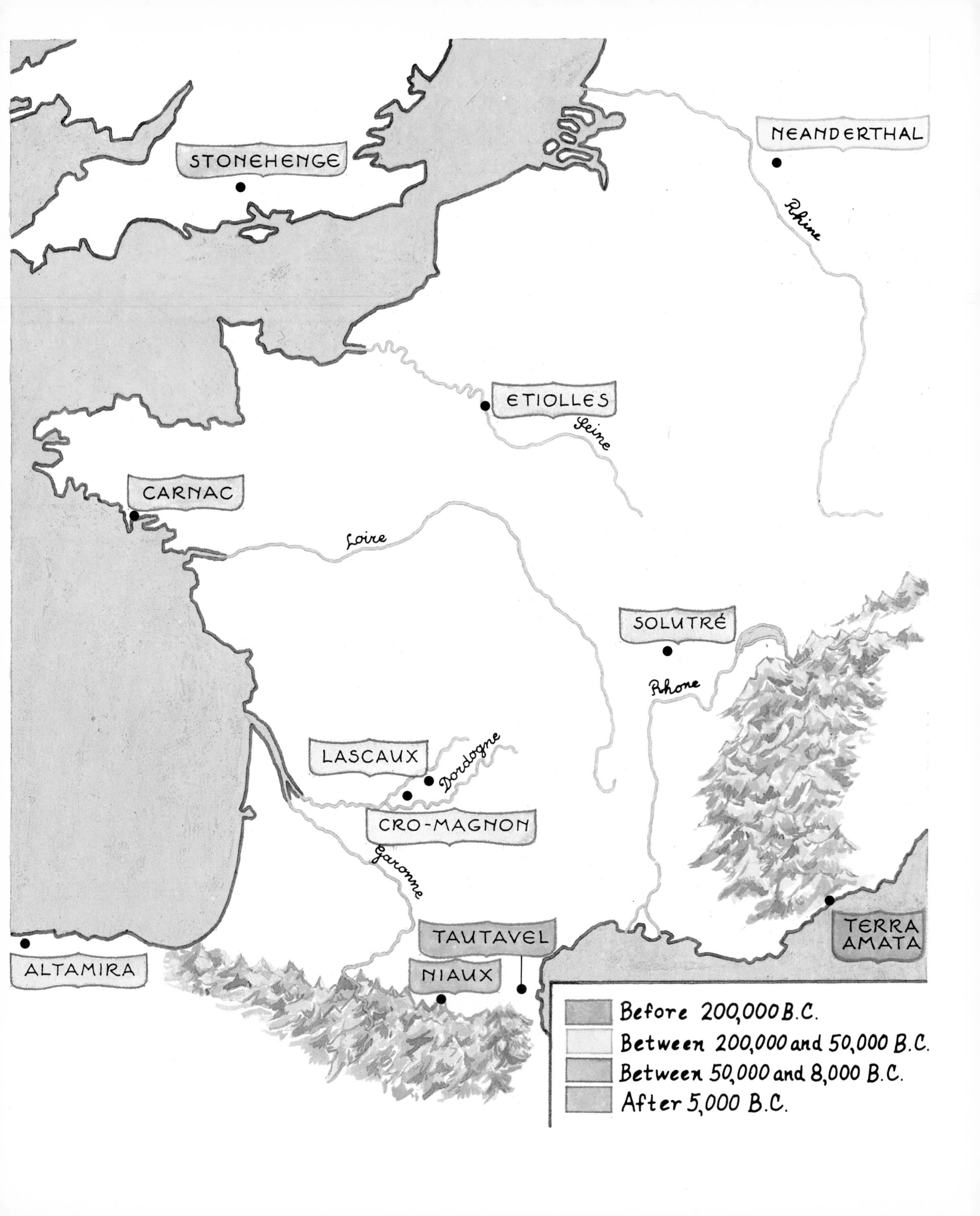
NEANDERTHAL
STONEHENGE
Rhine
ETIOLLES
Seine
CARNAC
Loire
SOLUTRÉ
Rhone
LASCAUX
Dordogne
CRO-MAGNON
Garonne
TAUTAVEL
TERRA AMATA
ALTAMIRA
NIAUX
Before 200,000 B.C.
Between 200,000 and 50,000 B.C.
Between 50,000 and 8,000 B.C.
After 5,000 B.C.

1 2 3 4 5 6 7 8 9 10—WOR—93 92 91 90 89 88 87 86 85